The Tao

The Gospel of Thomas
and the
Tao Te Ching

A Comparative Study by
Joseph B. Lumpkin

For information about first time authors, contact Fifth Estate, Post Office Box 116, Blountsville, AL 35031.

First Edition

Edited by Joyce A. Dujardin
Cover Designed by Matt Owens

Printed on acid-free paper

Library of Congress Control No: 2005922074

ISBN: 0-9760992-6-8

Fifth Estate, 2005

Dedication

To my friend and fellow traveler, Lisa Ryan;

It has taken fifty years for me to realize:

When we have become detached we can see clearly;

When we give birth to our real self we are saved.

You have been patient with me.

Thank you.

Jesus said: Become passers-by.

Jesus said: If you bring forth what is within you, it will save you. If you do not have it within you to bring forth, that which you lack will destroy you.

Introduction

In the winter of 1945, in Upper Egypt, an Arab peasant was gathering fertilizer and topsoil for his crops. While digging in the soft dirt he came across a large earthen vessel. Inside were scrolls containing hitherto unseen books.

The scrolls were discovered near the site of the ancient town of Chenoboskion, at the base of a mountain named Gebel et-Tarif, near Hamra-Dum, in the vicinity of Naj 'Hammadi, about sixty miles from Luxor in Egypt. The texts were written in the Coptic language and preserved on papyrus sheets. The lettering style dated them as having been penned around the third or fourth century A.D. The Gospel of Thomas is the longest of the volumes consisting of between 114 and 118 verses. Recent study indicates that the original works, of which the scrolls are copies, may predate the four canonical gospels of Matthew, Mark, Luke, and John. The origin of The Gospel of Thomas is now thought to be from the first or second century A.D.

The peasant boy who found this treasure stood to be rewarded greatly. This could have been the discovery of a lifetime for his family, but the boy had no idea what he had. He took the scrolls home, where his mother burned some as kindling. Others were sold to the black market antique dealers in Cairo. It would be years until they found their way into the hands of a scholar. Part of the thirteenth codex was smuggled from Egypt to America. In 1955 the existence of the codex had reached the ears of Gilles Quispel, a professor of religion and history in the Netherlands. The race was on to find and translate the scrolls.

The introduction of the collected sayings of Jesus refers to the writer as "Didymus (Jude) Thomas." This is the same Thomas who doubted Jesus and was then told to place his hand within the breach in the side of the Savior. In the Gospel of St. John, he is referred to as "Didymus," which means "twin" in Greek. In Aramaic, the name "Jude" (or Judas) also carries the sense of "twin". The use of this title led some in the apocryphal tradition to believe that he was the brother and confidant of Jesus. However, when applied to Jesus himself, the literal meaning of "twin" must be rejected by orthodox Christianity as well as anyone adhering to the doctrine of the virgin birth of the only begotten son of God. The title is likely meant to signify that Thomas was a close confidant of Jesus.

Ancient church historians mention that Thomas preached to the Parthians in Persia and it is said he was buried in Edessa. Fourth century chronicles attribute the evangelization of India (Asia-Minor or Central Asia) to Thomas.

The texts, which some believe predate the four gospels, has a very Zen-like or Eastern flavor. Since it is widely held that the four gospels of Matthew, Mark, Luke, and John have a common reference in the basic text of Mark, it stands to reason that all follow the same general insight and language. Since scholars believe that the Gospel of Thomas predates the four main gospels, it can be assumed it was written outside the influences common to the other gospels. Although the codex found in Egypt is dated to the fourth century, the actual construction of the text of Thomas is placed by most Biblical scholars at about 70 – 150 A.D.

If Thomas wrote his gospel first, without input from Mark, and from the standpoint of Eastern exposure as a result of his sojourn into India, it could explain the "Eastern" quality of the text.

Moreover, there is some speculation that the sayings found in Thomas could be more accurate to the original intent and wording of Jesus than the other gospels. This may seem counter-intuitive until we realize that Christianity itself is an Eastern religion, albeit Middle-Eastern. Although, as it spread west the faith went through many changes to westernize or Romanize it…Jesus was both mystical and Middle-Eastern.

The Gospel of Thomas was most likely composed in Syria, where tradition holds the church of Edessa was founded by Judas Thomas, "The Twin" (Didymos). The gospel may well be the earliest written tradition in the Syriac church

The Gospel of Thomas is sometimes called a Gnostic gospel. The term "Gnostic" derives from "gnosis," which in Greek means "knowledge." Gnostics believed that knowledge is formed or found from a personal encounter with God brought about by inward or intuitive insight. They believed they were privy to a secret knowledge about the divine. It is this knowledge that leads to their name. It is possible that the roots of the Gnostic system pre-dates Christianity and found a suitable home in the mystical side of the Christian faith.

There are numerous references to the Gnostics in second century literature. Their form of Christianity was considered heresy by the early church fathers. It is from the writings condemning the group that we glean most of our information. They are alluded to in the Bible in 1 Tm 1:4 and 1 Tm 6:20, and possibly the entirety of Jude, as the writers of the Bible defended their theology against that of the Gnostics.

It is because of the Eastern tone of Thomas, the Gnostic theology embedded in Thomas, and the possible Pre-Christian influence of the text that makes it so compatible with the philosophy of the Tao Te Ching, so as to make one a fascinating supplement to the other. Both advance inner and intuitive knowledge above all. Both allude to the way to acquire this knowledge through an unwavering search within oneself.

The Tao Te Ching was written by a man referred to as Lao Tzu. The unknown author's name means both "the old philosopher" and "the old philosophy." Hence Lao Tzu may also be the title for the book or the name or title of the author.

Lao Tzu lived in ancient China and was the keeper of the Imperial Library. Legends tell us he was famous for his wisdom. He was an advocate for personal inner growth, moral government, and the rights of the people. Perceiving the growing corruption of the government, he left for the countryside. On his way, the guard at the city gates asked Lao Tzu to write out his teachings for the benefit of future generations. Lao Tzu wrote the Tao Te Ching, and was never heard of again. The Tao Te Ching is the fundamental text of Taoism.

Taoism is a philosophy based upon the search for a middle path through life; avoiding extremes so that no act is followed by a reaction. This philosophy has come to influence many other aspects of Eastern life; including martial arts in such styles as Tai Chi, Aikido, Shinsei Hapkido, Jujutsu, and Judo. The concept of balancing the masculine and feminine or hard and soft applied also in Eastern medicines such as herbology and acupuncture.

The practice of Taoism is principally concerned with discovering balance and self-knowledge. All things, actions, and even intents, are broken into positive and negative, or masculine and feminine influences. Taoism advocates learning to sense the world directly, to "intuit" the flow of things, and to maintain a balance of opposing forces.

In doing so, one must contemplate impressions deeply as one attempts to become detached, without resorting to coloring intuitive impressions with personal expectations. Taoism advises against relying on ideologies, because to do so will rob one's life of its meaning and personal intuition. By developing intuition, one acquires a deeper understanding of the world, one's place, and the future. Lao Tzu remarked that an excessive force tends to trigger an opposing force, and therefore the use of force cannot be the basis for establishing a strong and lasting social foundation of control, life, or government. The force used to lead others is said to be the "moral force," virtue, or wisdom of the Master.

There seem to be two theories disputing the dating of the Tao Te Ching. According to tradition, the work originates in the fourth century B.C., but recent discoveries confirm that the writings originate no earlier than the third or fourth century B.C. The oldest existing copy is from 206 or 195 B.C.

The second hypothesis concludes that the teaching may be old enough to pre-date the invention of paper. In fact, its form exhibits many of the features of an oral tradition, suggesting it may pre-date writing as well. Oral traditions are very difficult to trace and we may never know how old the verses are.

The Tao Te Ching as it exists today, consists of 81 short chapters among which 37 form the first part, *the Book of the Way* (Tao), and the next 44 form *the Book of Te* ("Te" is a word translated by James Legge as "virtue", pointing to the *Tao of Heaven*). Its division into chapters is considered to be the result of the remarks of Heschang Gong (Han dynasty). Other traditional interpretations conclude the name may be "The Book of the Way of Virtue" or "The Book of Flow and Harmony." It is in the association of intuition, insight, and the inward knowledge leading to God that the Gospel of Thomas and the Tao Te Ching come together to give the reader a most amazing experience.

Thus, in the Gnostic words of Thomas and the philosophical Taoism of Lao Tzu, we find a melding of East and West that brings together what is best in both worlds; wisdom, peace, and balance.

The translations of both The Gospel of Thomas and the Tao Te Ching presented herein are the result of a gestalt brought about by contrasting and comparing all of the foremost translations, where the best phrasing was chosen to follow the intent and meaning of the text. Both books are presented so they may be viewed and studied together.

In the document to follow, the Gospel of Thomas will appear as a bold text. If there are other relevant but divergent interpretations of phrases in Thomas, they are included in parenthesis. Any parallels of text or meaning that appear in the Bible are placed below the verse in italicized plain text. All verses from the Tao Te Ching will be in an oriental style text. In this way the reader can easily identify which body of work is being referenced and observe how they fit together.

It was first thought that we should print verses of similar meaning from the Tao Te Ching following those of Thomas. However, after many hours of work it became obvious that the texts are linked on an intuitive level. This meant the number of verses that could be matched became too numerous and fluid. The project became unmanageable. Thus, it was decided that the reader should be allowed to draw direct connections between the Gospel of Thomas and the Tao Te Ching by letting them stand on their own. In this way, the reader is free to associate those verses which may seem connected at the time, according to the need and mindset.

Since the deeper meanings of both Thomas and the Tao Te Ching are both direct and indirect, it is hoped that each time they are read some new insight and treasure can be taken from them.

THE GOSPEL OF THOMAS

These are the secret sayings which the living Jesus has spoken and Judas who is also Thomas (the twin) (Didymos Judas Thomas) wrote.

1. And he said: Whoever finds the interpretation of these sayings will not taste death.

John 8:51 Very truly I tell you, whoever keeps my word will never see death.

2. Jesus said: Let he who seeks not stop seeking until he finds, and when he finds he will be troubled, and when he has been troubled he will marvel (be astonished) and he will reign over all and in reigning, he will find rest.

3. Jesus said: If those who lead you said to you: Behold, the Kingdom is in the sky, then the birds of the sky would enter before you. If they said to you: It is in the sea, then the fish of the sea would enter ahead you. But the Kingdom of God

exists within you and it exists outside of you. Those who come to know (recognize) themselves will find it, and when you come to know yourselves you will become known and you will realize that you are the children of the Living Father. Yet if you do not come to know yourselves then you will dwell in poverty and it will be you who are that poverty.

Luke 17:20 And when he was demanded of by the Pharisees, when the kingdom of God should come, he answered them and said, The kingdom of God cometh not with observation: Neither shall they say, Lo here! Lo There! For, behold, the kingdom of God is within you.

4. Jesus said: The person of old age will not hesitate to ask a little child of seven days about the place of life, and he will live. For many who are first will become last, (and the last will be first). And they will become one and the same.

Mark 9:35 He sat down, called the twelve, and said to them: Whoever wants to be first must be last of all and servant of all. 36 Then he took a little child and put it among them, and taking it in his arms, he said to them: 37 Whoever welcomes one such child in my name welcomes me, and whoever welcomes me welcomes not me but the one who sent me.

5. Jesus said: Recognize what is in front of your face, and what has been hidden from you will be revealed to you. For there is nothing hidden which will not be revealed (become manifest), and nothing buried that will not be raised.

Mark 4:2 For there is nothing hid, except to be made manifest; nor is anything secret, except to come to light.

Luke 12:3 Nothing is covered up that will not be revealed, or hidden that will not be known.

Matthew 10:26 So have no fear of them; for nothing is covered up that will not be uncovered, and nothing secret that will not become known.

6. His Disciples asked Him, they said to him: How do you want us to fast, and how will we pray? And how will we be charitable (give alms), and what laws of diet will we maintain?

Jesus said: Do not lie, and do not practice what you hate, for everything is in the plain sight of Heaven. For there is nothing concealed that will not become manifest, and there is nothing covered that will not be exposed.

Luke 11:1 He was praying in a certain place, and after he had finished, one of his disciples said to him, Lord, teach us to pray, as John taught his disciples.

7. Jesus said: Blessed is the lion that the man will eat, for the lion will become the man. Cursed is the man that the lion shall eat, and still the lion will become man.

Mathew 26:20-30 He who dipped his hand with me in the dish, the same will betray me. The Son of Man goes, even as it is written of him, but woe to that man through whom the Son of Man is betrayed! It would be better for that man if he had not been born. Judas, who betrayed him, answered, It isn't me, is it, Rabbi? He said to him, You said it. As they were eating, Jesus took bread, gave thanks for it, and broke it. He gave to the disciples, and said, Take, eat; this is my body. He took the cup, gave thanks, and gave to them, saying: All of you drink it, for this is my blood of the new covenant, which is poured out for many for the remission of sins. But I tell you that I will not drink of this fruit of the vine from now on, until that day when I drink it anew with you in my Father's Kingdom. When they had sung a hymn, they went out to the Mount of Olives.

8. And he said: The Kingdom of Heaven is like a wise fisherman who casts his net into the sea. He drew it up from the sea full of small fish. Among them he found a fine large fish. That wise fisherman threw all the small fish back into the sea and chose the large fish without hesitation. Whoever has ears to hear, let him hear!

Matthew 13:47 Again, the kingdom of heaven is like a net that was thrown into the sea and caught fish of every kind; 48 when it was full, they drew it ashore, sat down, and put the good into baskets but threw out the bad.

9. Jesus said: Now, the sower came forth. He filled his hand and threw (the seeds). Some fell upon the road and the birds came and gathered them up. Others fell on the stone and they did not take deep enough roots in the soil, and so did not produce grain. Others fell among the thorns and they choked

the seed, and the worm ate them. Others fell upon the good earth and it produced good fruit up toward the sky, it bore 60 fold and 120 fold.

Matthew 13:3 And he told them many things in parables, saying: Listen! A sower went out to sow. 4 And as he sowed, some seeds fell on the path, and the birds came and ate them up. 5 Other seeds fell on rocky ground, where they did not have much soil, and they sprang up quickly, since they had no depth of soil. 6 But when the sun rose, they were scorched; and since they had no root, they withered away. 7 Other seeds fell among thorns, and the thorns grew up and choked them. 8 Other seeds fell on good soil and brought forth grain, some a hundredfold, some sixty, some thirty.

Mark 4:2 And he taught them many things in parables, and in his teaching he said to them: 3 Behold! A sower went out to sow. 4 And as he sowed, some seed fell along the path, and the birds came and devoured it. 5 Other seed fell on rocky ground, where it had not much soil, and immediately it sprang up, since it had no depth of soil; 6 and when the sun rose it was scorched, and since it had no root it withered away. 7 Other seed fell among thorns and the thorns grew up and choked it, and it yielded no grain. 8 And other seeds fell into good soil and brought forth grain, growing up and increasing and yielding thirty fold and sixty fold and a hundredfold. 9 And he said, He who has ears to hear, let him hear.

Luke 8:4 And when a great crowd came together and people from town after town came to him, he said in a parable: 5 A sower went out to sow his seed; and as he sowed, some fell along the path, and was trodden under foot, and the birds of the air devoured it. 6 And some fell on the rock; and as it grew up, it withered away, because it had no moisture. 7 And some fell among thorns; and the thorns grew with it and choked it. 8 And some fell into good soil and grew, and yielded a hundredfold. As he said this, he called out, He who has ears to hear, let him hear.

10. Jesus said: I have cast fire upon the world and behold, I guard it until it is ablaze.

Luke 12:49 I came to bring fire to the earth, and how I wish it were already kindled.

11. Jesus said: This sky will pass away, and the one above it will pass away. The dead are not alive, and the living will not die. In the days when you consumed what is dead, you made it alive. When you come into the Light, what will you do? On the day when you were united (one), you became separated (two). When you have become separated (two), what will you do?

Matthew 24:35 Heaven and earth will pass away, but my words will not pass away.

12. The Disciples said to Jesus: We know that you will go away from us. Who is it that will be our teacher?

Jesus said to them: Wherever you are (in the place that you have come), you will go to James the Righteous, for whose sake Heaven and Earth were made (came into being).

13. Jesus said to his Disciples: Compare me to others, and tell me who I am like. Simon Peter said to him: You are like a righteous messenger (angel) of God. Matthew said to him: You are like a (wise) philosopher (of the heart). Thomas said

22

to him: Teacher, my mouth is not capable of saying who you are like!

Jesus said: I'm not your teacher, now that you have drunk; you have become drunk from the bubbling spring that I have tended (measured out). And he took him, and withdrew and spoke three words to him: "ahyh ashr ahyh" (I am Who I am).

Now when Thomas returned to his comrades, they inquired of him: What did Jesus said to you? Thomas said to them: If I tell you even one of the words which he spoke to me, you will take up stones and throw them at me, and fire will come from the stones to consume you.

Mark 8:27 Jesus went on with his disciples to the villages of Caesarea Philippi; and on the way he asked his disciples, Who do people say that I am? 28 And they answered him, John the Baptist; and others, Elijah; and still others, one of the prophets. 29 He asked them, But who do you say that I am? Peter answered him, You are the Messiah. 30 And he sternly ordered them not to tell anyone about him.

14. Jesus said to them: If you fast, you will give rise to transgression (sin) for yourselves. And if you pray, you will be condemned. And if you give alms, you will cause harm (evil) to your spirits. And when you go into the countryside, if they take you in (receive you) then eat what they set before you and heal the sick among them. For what goes into your mouth will not defile you, but rather what comes out of your mouth, that is what will defile you.

Luke 10:8 Whenever you enter a town and its people welcome you, eat what is set before you; 9 Cure the sick who are there, and say to them, The kingdom of God has come near to you.

Mark 7:15 There is nothing outside a person that by going in can defile, but the things that come out are what defile.

Matthew 15:11 Not that what goes into the mouth defiles a man, but what comes out of the mouth, this defiles a man.

▣▣

Romans 14.14 I know and am persuaded in the Lord Jesus that nothing is unclean in itself; but it is unclean for any one who thinks it unclean.

15. Jesus said: When you see him who was not born of woman, bow yourselves down upon your faces and worship him for he is your Father.

16. Jesus said: People think perhaps I have come to spread peace upon the world. They do not know that I have come to cast dissention (conflict) upon the earth; fire, sword, war. For there will be five in a house. Three will be against two and two against three, the father against the son and the son against the father. And they will stand alone.

Matthew 10:34 Do not think that I have come to bring peace to the earth; I have not come to bring peace, but a sword. 35 For I have come to set a man against his father, and a daughter against her mother, and a daughter-in-law against her mother-in-law; 36 and one's foes will be members of one's own household.

Luke 12:51 Do you think that I have come to give peace on earth? No, I tell you, but rather division; 52 for henceforth in one house there will be five divided, three against two and two against three; 53 they will be divided, father against son and son against father, mother against daughter and daughter against her mother, mother-in-law against her daughter-in-law and daughter-in-law against her mother-in-law.

17. Jesus said: I will give to you what eye has not seen, what ear has not heard, what hand has not touched, and what has not occurred to the mind of man.

1 Cor 2:9 But, as it is written, What no eye has seen, nor ear heard, nor the human heart conceived, what God has prepared for those who love him.

18. The Disciples said to Jesus: Tell us how our end will come. Jesus said: Have you already discovered the beginning (origin), so that you inquire about the end? Where the beginning (origin) is, there the end will be. Blessed be he who will take his place in the beginning (stand at the origin) for he will know the end, and he will not experience death.

19. Jesus said: Blessed is he who came into being before he came into being. If you become my Disciples and heed my sayings, these stones will serve you. For there are five trees in paradise for you, which are undisturbed in summer and in winter and their leaves do not fall. Whoever knows them will not experience death.

20. The Disciples said to Jesus: Tell us what the Kingdom of Heaven is like. He said to them: It is like a mustard seed, smaller than all other seeds and yet when it falls on the tilled earth, it produces a great plant and becomes shelter for the birds of the sky.

Mark 4:30 He also said, With what can we compare the kingdom of God, or what parable will we use for it? 31 It is like a mustard seed, which, when sown upon the ground, is the smallest of all the seeds on earth; 32 yet when it is sown it grows up and becomes the greatest of all shrubs, and puts forth large branches, so that the birds of the air can make nests in its shade.

Matthew 13:31 The kingdom of heaven is like a grain of mustard seed which a man took and sowed in his field; 32 it is the smallest of all seeds, but when it has grown it is the greatest of shrubs and becomes a tree, so that the birds of the air come and make nests in its branches.

Luke 13.18 He said therefore, What is the kingdom of God like? And to what shall I compare it? 19 It is like a grain of mustard seed which a man took and sowed in his garden; and it grew and became a tree, and the birds of the air made nests in its branches.

21. Mary said to Jesus: Who are your Disciples like? He said: They are like little children who are living in a field that is not theirs. When the owners of the field come, they will say: Let us have our field! It is as if they were naked in front of them (They undress in front of them in order to let them have what is theirs) and they give back the field. Therefore I said, if the owner of the house knows that the thief is coming, he will be alert before he arrives and will not allow him to dig through into the house to carry away his belongings. You, must be on guard and beware of the world (system). Prepare yourself (arm yourself) with great strength or the bandits will find a way to reach you, for the problems you expect will come. Let there be among you a person of understanding

(awareness). When the crop ripened, he came quickly with his sickle in his hand to reap. Whoever has ears to hear, let him hear!

Matthew 24:43 But understand this: if the owner of the house had known in what part of the night the thief was coming, he would have stayed awake and would not have let his house be broken into.

Mark 4:26 He also said, The kingdom of God is as if someone would scatter seed on the ground, 27 and would sleep and rise night and day, and the seed would sprout and grow, he does not know how. 28 The earth produces of itself, first the stalk, then the head, then the full grain in the head. 29 But when the grain is ripe, at once he goes in with his sickle, because the harvest has come.

Luke 12:39 But know this, that if the householder had known at what hour the thief was coming, he would not have left his house to be broken into. 40 You also must be ready; for the Son of man is coming at an unexpected hour.

22. Jesus saw little children who were being suckled. He said to his Disciples: These little children who are being suckled are like those who enter the Kingdom.

They said to him: Should we become like little children in order to enter the Kingdom?

Jesus said to them: When you make the two one, and you make the inside as the outside and the outside as the inside, when you make the above as the below, and if you make the male and the female one and the same (united male and female) so that the man will not be masculine (male) and the female be not feminine (female), when you establish an eye in the place of an eye and a hand in the place of a hand and a foot in the place of a foot and an likeness (image) in the place of a likeness (an image), then will you enter the Kingdom.

Luke 18:16 But Jesus called for them and said, Let the little children come to me, and do not stop them; for it is to such as these that the kingdom of God belongs. 17 Truly I tell you, whoever does not receive the kingdom of God as a little child will never enter it.

Mark 9:43 If your hand causes you to stumble, cut it off; it is better for you to enter life maimed than to have two hands and to go to hell, to the unquenchable fire. 45 And if your foot causes you to stumble, cut it off; it is better for you to enter life lame than to have two feet and to be thrown into hell. 47 And if your eye causes you to stumble, tear it out; it is better for you to enter the kingdom of God with one eye than to have two eyes and to be thrown into hell, 48 where their worm never dies, and the fire is never quenched.

Matthew 18:3 And said, Verily, I say unto you, unless you turn and become like children, you will never enter the kingdom of heaven. 4 Whoever humbles himself like this child, he is the greatest in the kingdom of heaven. 5 Whoever receives one such child in my name receives me;

Matthew 5:29 If your right eye causes you to sin, pluck it out and throw it away; it is better that you lose one of your members than that your whole body be thrown into hell. 30 And if your right hand causes you to sin, cut it off and throw it away; it is better that you lose one of your members than that your whole body go into hell.

23. Jesus said: I will choose you, one out of a thousand and two out of ten thousand and they will stand as a single one.

24. His Disciples said: Show us the place where you are (your place), for it is necessary for us to seek it.

He said to them: Whoever has ears, let him hear! Within a man of light there is light, and he illumines the entire world. If he does not shine, he is darkness (there is darkness).

John13:36 Simon Peter said to him, Lord, where are you going? Jesus answered, Where I am going, you cannot follow me now; but you will follow afterward.

Matthew 6:22 The eye is the lamp of the body. So, if your eye is healthy, your whole body will be full of light; 23 but if your eye is unhealthy, your whole body will be full of darkness. If then the light in you is darkness, how great is the darkness!

🔲🔲🔲

Luke 11:34 Your eye is the lamp of your body; when your eye is sound, your whole body is full of light; but when it is not sound, your body is full of darkness. 35 Therefore be careful lest the light in you be darkness. 36 If then your whole body is full of light, having no part dark, it will be wholly bright, as when a lamp with its rays gives you light.

25. Jesus said: Love your friend (Brother) as your soul; protect him as you would the pupil of your own eye.

26. Jesus said: You see the speck in your brother's eye but the beam that is in your own eye you do not see. When you remove the beam out of your own eye, then will you see clearly to remove the speck out of your brother's eye.

Matthew 7:3 Why do you see the speck in your neighbor's eye, but do not notice the log in your own eye? 4 Or how can you say to your neighbor, Let me take the speck out of your eye, while the log is in your own eye? 5 You hypocrite, first take the log out of your own eye, and then you will see clearly to take the speck out of your neighbor's eye.

Luke 6:41 Why do you see the speck that is in your brother's eye, but do not notice the log that is in your own eye? 42 Or how can you say to your brother, Brother, let me take out the speck that is in your eye, when you yourself do not see the log that is in your own eye? You hypocrite, first take the log out of your own eye, and then you will see clearly to take out the speck that is in your brother's eye.

27. Jesus said: Unless you fast from the world (system), you will not find the Kingdom of God. Unless you keep the Sabbath (entire week) as Sabbath, you will not see the Father.

28. Jesus said: I stood in the midst of the world. In the flesh I appeared to them. I found them all drunk; I found none thirsty among them. My soul grieved for the sons of men, for they are blind in their hearts and do not see that they came into the world empty they are destined (determined) to leave the world empty. However, now they are drunk. When they have shaken off their wine, then they will repent (change their ways).

29. Jesus said: If the flesh came into being because of spirit,

it is a marvel, but if spirit came into being because of the body, it would be a marvel of marvels. I marvel indeed at how great wealth has taken up residence in this poverty.

30. Jesus said: Where there are three gods, they are gods (Where there are three gods they are without god). Where there is only one, I say that I am with him. Lift the stone and there you will find me, Split the wood and there am I.

Matthew 18:20 For where two or three are gathered in my name, I am there among them.

31. Jesus said: No prophet is accepted in his own village, no physician heals those who know him.

Mark 6:4 Then Jesus said to them, Prophets are not without honor, except in their hometown, and among their own kin, and in their own house.

Matthew 13:57 And they took offense at him. But Jesus said to them: A prophet is not without honor save in his own country and in his own house.

Luke 4:24 And he said, Truly, I say to you, no prophet is acceptable in his own country.

John 4:43 After the two days he departed to Galilee. 44 For Jesus himself testified that a prophet has no honor in his own country.

32. Jesus said: A city being built (and established) upon a high mountain and fortified cannot fall nor can it be hidden.

Matthew 5:14 You are the light of the world. A city built on a hill cannot be hid.

33. Jesus said: What you will hear in your ear preach from your rooftops. For no one lights a lamp and sets it under a basket nor puts it in a hidden place, but rather it is placed up a lamp-stand so that everyone who comes and goes will see its light.

Matthew 10:27 What I say to you in the dark, tell in the light; and what you hear whispered, proclaim from the housetops.

Luke 8:16 No one after lighting a lamp hides it under a jar, or puts it under a bed, but puts it on a lamp stand, so that those who enter may see the light.

Matthew 5:15 Nor do men light a lamp and put it under a bushel, but on a stand, and it gives light to all in the house.

Mark 4:21 And he said to them, Is a lamp brought in to be put under a bushel, or under a bed, and not on a stand?

Luke 11:33 No one after lighting a lamp puts it in a cellar or under a bushel, but on a stand, that those who enter may see the light.

34. Jesus said: If a blind person leads a blind person, both fall into a pit.

Matthew 15:14 Let them alone; they are blind guides of the blind. And if one blind person guides another, both will fall into a pit.

Luke 6:39 He also told them a parable: Can a blind man lead a blind man? Will they not both fall into a pit?

35. Jesus said: It is impossible for anyone to enter the house of a strong man to take it by force unless he binds his hands, then he will be able to loot his house.

Matthew 12:29 Or how can one enter a strong man's house and plunder his goods, unless he first binds the strong man? Then indeed he may plunder his house.

Luke 11:21 When a strong man, fully armed, guards his own palace, his goods are in peace; 22 but when one stronger than he assails him and overcomes him, he takes away his armor in which he trusted, and divides his spoil.

Mark 3:27 But no one can enter a strong man's house and plunder his property without first tying up the strong man; then indeed the house can be plundered.

▣▣▣

36. Jesus said: Do not worry from morning to evening nor from evening to morning about the food that you will eat nor about what clothes you will wear. You are much superior to the Lilies which neither card nor spin. When you have no clothing, what do you wear? Who can add time to your life (increase your stature)? He himself will give to you your garment.

Matthew 6:25 Therefore I tell you, do not worry about your life, what you will eat or what you will drink, or about your body, what you will wear. Is not life more than food, and the body more than clothing? 26 Look at the birds of the air; they neither sow nor reap nor gather into barns, and yet your heavenly Father feeds them. Are you not of more value than they? 27 And can any of you by worrying add a single hour to your span of life? 28 And why do you worry about clothing? Consider the lilies of the field, how they grow; they neither toil nor spin, 29 yet I tell you, even Solomon in all his glory was not clothed like one of these. 30 But if God so clothes the grass of the field, which is alive today and tomorrow is thrown into the oven, will he not much more clothe you--you of little faith? 31 Therefore do not worry, saying, What will we eat? or What will we drink? or What will we wear?

Luke 12:22 And he said to his disciples, Therefore I tell you, do not be anxious about your life, what you shall eat, nor about your body, what you shall put on. 23 For life is more than food, and the body more than clothing.

37. His Disciples said: When will you appear to us, and when will we see you?

Jesus said: When you take off your garments without being ashamed, and place your garments under your feet and tread on them as the little children do, then will you see the Son of the Living-One, and you will not be afraid.

38. Jesus said: Many times have you yearned to hear these sayings which I speak to you, and you have no one else from whom to hear them. There will be days when you will seek me but you will not find me.

39. Jesus said: The Pharisees and the Scribes have received the keys of knowledge, but they have hidden them. They did not go in, nor did they permit those who wished to enter to

do so. However, you be as wise (astute) as serpents and innocent as doves.

Luke 11:52 Woe to you lawyers! For you have taken away the key of knowledge; you did not enter yourselves, and you hindered those who were entering.

Matthew 10:16 See, I am sending you out like sheep into the midst of wolves; so be wise as serpents and innocent as doves.

Matthew 23.13 But woe unto you, scribes and Pharisees, hypocrites! because you shut the kingdom of heaven against men; for you neither enter yourselves, nor allow those who would enter to go in.

40. Jesus said: A grapevine has been planted outside the (vineyard of the) Father, and since it is not viable (supported) it will be pulled up by its roots and destroyed.

Matthew 15:13 He answered, Every plant that my heavenly Father has not planted will be uprooted.

41. Jesus said: Whoever has (it) in his hand, to him will (more) be given. And whoever does not have, from him will be taken even the small amount which he has.

Matthew 25:29 For to all those who have, more will be given, and they will have an abundance; but from those who have nothing, even what they have will be taken away.

Luke 19:26 I tell you, that to every one who has will more be given; but from him who has not, even what he has will be taken away.

42. Jesus said: Become passers-by.

43. His Disciples said to him: Who are you, that you said these things to us?

Jesus said to them: You do not recognize who I am from what I said to you, but rather you have become like the Jews who either love the tree and hate its fruit, or love the fruit and hate the tree.

John 8:25 They said to him, Who are you? Jesus said to them, Why do I speak to you at all?

Matthew 7:16 You will know them by their fruits. Are grapes gathered from thorns, or figs from thistles? 17 In the same way, every good tree bears good fruit, but the bad tree bears bad fruit. 18 A good tree cannot bear bad fruit, nor can a bad tree bear good fruit. 19 Every tree that does not bear good fruit is cut down and thrown into the fire. 20 Thus you will know them by their fruits.

44. Jesus said: Whoever blasphemes against the Father, it will be forgiven him. And whoever blasphemes against the Son, it will be forgiven him. Yet whoever blasphemes against the Holy Spirit, it will not be forgiven him neither on earth nor in heaven.

Mark 3:28 Truly I tell you, people will be forgiven for their sins and whatever blasphemies they utter; 29 but whoever blasphemes against the Holy Spirit can never have forgiveness, but is guilty of an eternal sin.

Matthew 12:31 Therefore I tell you, every sin and blasphemy will be forgiven men, but the blasphemy against the Spirit will not be forgiven. 32 And whoever says a word against the Son of man will be forgiven; but whoever speaks against the Holy Spirit will not be forgiven, either in this age or in the age to come.

Luke 12:10 And every one who speaks a word against the Son of man will be forgiven; but he who blasphemes against the Holy Spirit will not be forgiven.

45. Jesus said: Grapes are not harvested from thorns, nor are figs gathered from thistles, for they do not give fruit. A good person brings forth goodness out of his storehouse. A bad person brings forth evil out of his evil storehouse which is in his heart, and he speaks evil, for out of the abundance of the heart he brings forth evil.

Luke 6:43 For no good tree bears bad fruit, nor again does a bad tree bear good fruit; 44 for each tree is known by its own fruit. For figs are not gathered from thorns, nor are grapes picked from a bramble

44

bush. 45 *The good man out of the good treasure of his heart produces good, and the evil man out of his evil treasure produces evil; for out of the abundance of the heart his mouth speaks.*

46. Jesus said: From Adam until John the Baptist there is none born of women who surpasses John the Baptist, so that his eyes should not be downcast (lowered). Yet I have said that whoever among you becomes like a child will know the Kingdom, and he will be greater than John.

Matthew 11:11 Truly I tell you, among those born of women no one has arisen greater than John the Baptist; yet the least in the kingdom of heaven is greater than he.

Luke 7:28 I tell you, among those born of women none is greater than John; yet he who is least in the kingdom of God is greater than he.

Matthew 18:2 He called a child, whom he put among them, 3 and said, Truly I tell you, unless you change and become like children, you will never enter the kingdom of heaven. 18:4 Whoever becomes humble like this child is the greatest in the kingdom of heaven.

47. Jesus said: It is impossible for a man to mount two horses or to draw two bows, and a servant cannot serve two masters, otherwise he will honor the one and disrespect the other. No man drinks vintage wine and immediately desires to drink new wine, and they do not put new wine into old wineskins or they would burst, and they do not put vintage wine into new wineskins or it would spoil (sour). They do not sew an old patch on a new garment because that would cause a split.

Matthew 6:24 No one can serve two masters; for a slave will either hate the one and love the other, or be devoted to the one and despise the other. You cannot serve God and wealth.

Matthew 9:16 No one sews a piece of unshrunk cloth on an old cloak, for the patch pulls away from the cloak, and a worse tear is made. 17 Neither is new wine put into old wineskins; otherwise, the skins burst, and the wine is spilled, and the skins are destroyed; but new wine is put into fresh wineskins, and so both are preserved.

Mark 2:21 *No one sews a piece of unshrunk cloth on an old garment; if he does, the patch tears away from it, the new from the old, and a worse tear is made. 22 And no one puts new wine into old wineskins; if he does, the wine will burst the skins, and the wine is lost, and so are the skins; but new wine is for fresh skins.*

Luke 5:36 *He told them a parable also: No one tears a piece from a new garment and puts it upon an old garment; if he does, he will tear the new, and the piece from the new will not match the old. 37 And no one puts new wine into old wineskins; if he does, the new wine will burst the skins and it will be spilled, and the skins will be destroyed. 38 But new wine must be put into fresh wineskins. 39 And no one after drinking old wine desires new; for he says, The old is good.*

48. Jesus said: If two make peace with each other in this one house, they will say to the mountain: Be moved! and it will be moved.

Matthew 18:19 *Again, truly I tell you, if two of you agree on earth about anything you ask, it will be done for you by my Father in heaven.*

Mark 11:23 Truly I tell you, if you say to this mountain, Be taken up and thrown into the sea, and if you do not doubt in your heart, but believe that what you say will come to pass, it will be done for you. 24 So I tell you, whatever you ask for in prayer, believe that you have received it, and it will be yours.

Matthew 17:20 He said to them, Because of your little faith. For truly, I say to you, if you have faith as a grain of mustard seed, you will say to this mountain, Move from here to there, and it will move; and nothing will be impossible to you.

49. Jesus said: Blessed is the solitary and chosen, for you will find the Kingdom. You have come from it, and unto it you will return.

50. Jesus said: If they said to you: From where do you come? Say to them: We have come from the Light, the place where the Light came into existence of its own accord and he stood and appeared in their image. If they said to you: Is it you? (Who are you?), say: We are his Sons and we are the

chosen of the Living Father. If they ask you: What is the sign of your Father in you? Say to them: It is movement with rest.

51. His Disciples said to him: When will the rest of the dead occur, and when will the New World come? He said to them: That which you look for has already come, but you do not recognize it.

52. His Disciples said to him: Twenty-four prophets preached in Israel, and they all spoke of (in) you. He said to them: You have ignored the Living-One who is in your presence and you have spoken only of the dead.

53. His Disciples said to him: Is circumcision beneficial or not? He said to them: If it were beneficial, their father would beget them already circumcised from their mother. However, the true spiritual circumcision has become entirely beneficial.

54. Jesus said: Blessed be the poor, for yours is the Kingdom of the Heaven.

Matthew 6:20 Then he looked up at his disciples and said: Blessed are you who are poor, for yours is the kingdom of God.

Luke 6:20 And he lifted up his eyes on his disciples, and said: Blessed are you poor, for yours is the kingdom of God.

Matthew 5:3 Blessed are the poor in spirit, for theirs is the kingdom of heaven.

55. Jesus said: Whoever does not hate his father and his mother will not be able to become my Disciple. And whoever does not hate his brothers and his sisters and does not take up his own cross in my way, will not become worthy of me.

Matthew 10:37 Whoever loves father or mother more than me is not worthy of me; and whoever loves son or daughter more than me is not worthy of me; 38 and whoever does not take up the cross and follow me is not worthy of me.

Luke 14:26 If any one comes to me and does not hate his own father and mother and wife and children and brothers and sisters, yes, and even his own life, he cannot be my disciple. 27 Whoever does not bear his own cross and come after me, cannot be my disciple.

56. Jesus said: Whoever has come to understand the world (system) has found a corpse, and whoever has found a corpse, is superior to the world (of him the system is not worthy).

57. Jesus said: The Kingdom of the Father is like a person who has good seed. His enemy came by night and sowed a weed among the good seed. The man did not permit them to pull up the weed, he said to them: perhaps you will intend to pull up the weed and you pull up the wheat along with it. But, on the day of harvest the weeds will be very visible and then they will pull them and burn them.

Matthew 13:24 He put before them another parable: The kingdom of heaven may be compared to someone who sowed good seed in his field; 25 but while everybody was asleep, an enemy came and sowed weeds among the wheat, and then went away. 26 So when the plants came up and bore grain, then the weeds appeared as well. 27 And the slaves of the householder came and said to him, Master, did you not sow good seed in your field? Where, then, did these weeds come from? 28 He answered, An enemy has done this. The slaves said to him, Then do you want us to go and gather them? 29 But he replied, No; for in gathering the weeds you would uproot the wheat along with them. 30 Let both of them grow together until the harvest; and at harvest time I will tell the reapers, Collect the weeds first and bind them in bundles to be burned, but gather the wheat into my barn.

58. Jesus said: Blessed is the person who has suffered, for he has found life. (Blessed is he who has suffered [to find life] and found life).

Matthew 11:28 Come to me, all you that are weary and are carrying heavy burdens, and I will give you rest.

59. Jesus said: Look to the Living-One while you are alive, otherwise, you might die and seek to see him and will be unable to find him.

John 7:34 You will search for me, but you will not find me; and where I am, you cannot come.

John 13:33 Little children, I am with you only a little longer. You will look for me; and as I said to the Jews so now I say to you, Where I am going, you cannot come.

60. They saw a Samaritan carrying a lamb, on his way to Judea. Jesus said to them: Why does he take the lamb with him? They said to him: So that he may kill it and eat it. He said to them: While it is alive he will not eat it, but only after he kills it and it becomes a corpse. They said: How could he do otherwise? He said to them: Look for a place of rest for yourselves, otherwise, you might become corpses and be eaten.

61. Jesus said: Two will rest on a bed and one will die and the other will live. Salome said: Who are you, man? As if sent by someone, you laid upon my bed and you ate from my table. Jesus said to her: "I-Am" he who is from that which is whole (the undivided). I have been given the things of my Father. Salome said: I'm your Disciple. Jesus said to her: Thus, I said that whenever someone is one (undivided)

he will be filled with light, yet whenever he is divided (chooses) he will be filled with darkness.

Luke 17:34 I tell you, on that night there will be two in one bed; one will be taken and the other left.

62. Jesus said: I tell my mysteries to those who are worthy of my mysteries. Do not let your right hand know what your left hand is doing.

Mark 4:11 And he said to them, To you has been given the secret of the kingdom of God, but for those outside, everything comes in parables.

Matthew 6:3 But when you give alms, do not let your left hand know what your right hand is doing.

Luke 8:10 He said, To you it has been given to know the secrets of the kingdom of God; but for others they are in parables, so that seeing they may not see, and hearing they may not understand.

Matthew 13:10 Then the disciples came and said to him, Why do you speak to them in parables? 11 And he answered them, To you it has been given to know the secrets of the kingdom of heaven, but to them it has not been given.

63. Jesus said: There was a wealthy person who had much money, and he said: I will use my money so that I may sow and reap and replant, to fill my storehouses with grain so that I lack nothing. This was his intention (is what he thought in his heart) but that same night he died. Whoever has ears, let him hear!

Luke 12:16 Then he told them a parable: The land of a rich man produced abundantly. 17 And he thought to himself, What should I do, for I have no place to store my crops? 18 Then he said, I will do this: I will pull down my barns and build larger ones, and there I will store all my grain and my goods. 19 And I will say to my soul, Soul, you have ample goods laid up for many years; relax, eat, drink, be merry. 20 But God said to him, You fool! This very night your life is being demanded of you. And the things you have prepared, whose will they be? 21 So it is with those who store up treasures for themselves but are not rich toward God.

64. Jesus said: A person had houseguests, and when he had prepared the banquet in their honor he sent his servant to invite the guests. He went to the first, he said to him: My master invites you. He replied: I have to do business with some merchants. They are coming to see me this evening. I will go to place my orders with them. I ask to be excused from the banquet. He went to another, he said to him: My master has invited you. He replied to him: I have just bought a house and they require me for a day. I will have no spare time. He came to another, he said to him: My master invites you. He replied to him: My friend is getting married and I must arrange a banquet for him. I will not be able to come. I ask to be excused from the banquet. He went to another, he said to him: My master invites you. He replied to him: I have bought a farm. I go to receive the rent. I will not be able to come. I ask to be excused. The servant returned, he said to his master: Those whom you have invited to the banquet have excused themselves. The master said to his servant: Go out to the roads, bring those whom you find so that they may feast.

▣▣

And he said: Businessmen and merchants will not enter the places of my Father.

Luke 14:16 Then Jesus said to him:, Someone gave a great dinner and invited many. 17 At the time for the dinner he sent his slave to say to those who had been invited, Come; for everything is ready now. 18 But they all alike began to make excuses. The first said to him, I have bought a piece of land, and I must go out and see it; please accept my regrets. 19 Another said, I have bought five yoke of oxen, and I am going to try them out; please accept my regrets. 20 Another said, I have just been married, and therefore I cannot come. 21 So the slave returned and reported this to his master. Then the owner of the house became angry and said to his slave, Go out at once into the streets and lanes of the town and bring in the poor, the crippled, the blind, and the lame. 22 And the slave said, Sir, what you ordered has been done, and there is still room. 23 Then the master said to the slave, Go out into the roads and lanes, and compel people to come in, so that my house may be filled. 24 For I tell you, none of those who were invited will taste my dinner.

Matthew 19:23 Then Jesus said to his disciples, Truly I tell you, it will be hard for a rich person to enter the kingdom of heaven.

Matthew 22:3 and sent his servants to call those who were invited to the marriage feast; but they would not come. 4 Again he sent other servants, saying, Tell those who are invited, Behold, I have made ready my dinner, my oxen and my fat calves are killed, and everything is ready; come to the marriage feast. 5 But they made light of it and went off, one to his farm, another to his business, 6 while the rest seized his servants, treated them shamefully, and killed them. 7 The king was angry, and he sent his troops and destroyed those murderers and burned their city. 8 Then he said to his servants, The wedding is ready, but those invited were not worthy. 9 Go therefore to the thoroughfares, and invite to the marriage feast as many as you find. 10 And those servants went out into the streets and gathered all whom they found, both bad and good; so the wedding hall was filled with guests. 11 But when the king came in to look at the guests, he saw there a man who had no wedding garment; 12 and he said to him, Friend, how did you get in here without a wedding garment? And he was speechless. 13 Then the king said to the attendants, Bind him hand and foot, and cast him into the outer darkness; there men will weep and gnash their teeth. 14 For many are called, but few are chosen.

65. He said: A kind person who owned a vineyard leased it to tenants so that they would work it and he would receive the fruit from them. He sent his servant so that the tenants would give to him the fruit of the vineyard. They seized his servant and beat him nearly to death. The servant went, he told his master what had happened. His master said: Perhaps they did not recognize him. So, he sent another servant. The tenants beat him also. Then the owner sent his son. He said: Perhaps they will respect my son. Since the tenants knew that he was the heir to the vineyard, they seized him and killed him. Whoever has ears, let him hear!

Matthew 21:33 Listen to another parable. There was a landowner who planted a vineyard, put a fence around it, dug a wine press in it, and built a watchtower. Then he leased it to tenants and went to another country. 34 When the harvest time had come, he sent his slaves to the tenants to collect his produce. 35 But the tenants seized his slaves and beat one, killed another, and stoned another. 36 Again he sent other slaves, more than the first; and they treated them in the same way. 37

Finally he sent his son to them, saying, They will respect my son. 38 But when the tenants saw the son, they said to themselves, This is the heir; come, let us kill him and get his inheritance. 39 So they seized him, threw him out of the vineyard, and killed him.

Mark 12:1 And he began to speak to them in parables. A man planted a vineyard, and set a hedge around it, and dug a pit for the wine press, and built a tower, and let it out to tenants, and went into another country. 2 When the time came, he sent a servant to the tenants, to get from them some of the fruit of the vineyard. 3 And they took him and beat him, and sent him away empty-handed. 4 Again he sent to them another servant, and they wounded him in the head, and treated him shamefully. 5 And he sent another, and him they killed; and so with many others, some they beat and some they killed. 6 He had still one other, a beloved son; finally he sent him to them, saying, They will respect my son. 7 But those tenants said to one another, This is the heir; come, let us kill him, and the inheritance will be ours. 8 And they took him and killed him, and cast him out of the vineyard. 9 What will the owner of the vineyard do? He will come and destroy the tenants, and give the vineyard to others.

Luke 20:9 And he began to tell the people this parable: A man planted a vineyard, and let it out to tenants, and went into another country for a long while. 10 When the time came, he sent a servant to the tenants, that they should give him some of the fruit of the vineyard; but the tenants beat him, and sent him away empty-handed. 11 And he sent another servant; him also they beat and treated shamefully, and sent him away empty-handed. 12 And he sent yet a third; this one they wounded and cast out. 13 Then the owner of the vineyard said, What shall I do? I will send my beloved son; it may be they will respect him. 14 But when the tenants saw him, they said to themselves, This is the heir; let us kill him, that the inheritance may be ours. 15 And they cast him out of the vineyard and killed him. What then will the owner of the vineyard do to them? 16 He will come and destroy those tenants, and give the vineyard to others. When they heard this, they said, God forbid!

66. Jesus said: Show me the stone which the builders have rejected. It is that one that is the cornerstone (keystone).

Matthew 21:42 Jesus said to them, Have you never read in the scriptures: The very stone which the builders rejected has become the head of the corner; this was the Lord's doing, and it is marvelous in our eyes?

Mark 12:10 Have you not read this scripture: The very stone which the builders rejected has become the head of the corner; 11 this was the Lord's doing, and it is marvelous in our eyes?

Luke 20:17 But he looked at them and said, What then does this text mean: The stone that the builders rejected has become the cornerstone?

67. Jesus said: Those who know everything but themselves, lack everything. (whoever knows the all and still feels a personal lacking, he is completely deficient).

68. Jesus said: Blessed are you when you are hated and persecuted, but they themselves will find no reason why you have been persecuted.

Matthew 5:11 Blessed are you when people revile you and persecute you and utter all kinds of evil against you falsely on my account.

Luke 6:22 Blessed are you when men hate you, and when they exclude you and revile you, and cast out your name as evil, on account of the Son of man!

69. Jesus said: Blessed are those who have been persecuted in their heart these are they who have come to know the Father in truth. Jesus said: Blessed are the hungry, for the stomach of him who desires to be filled will be filled.

Matthew 5:8 Blessed are the pure in heart, for they will see God.

Luke 6:21 Blessed are you who are hungry now, for you will be filled.

70. Jesus said: If you bring forth what is within you, it will save you. If you do not have it within you to bring forth, that which you lack will destroy you.

71. Jesus said: I will destroy this house, and no one will be able to build it again.

Mark 14:58 We heard him say, I will destroy this temple that is made with hands, and in three days I will build another, not made with hands.

72. A person said to him: Tell my brothers to divide the possessions of my father with me. He said to him: Oh man, who made me a divider? He turned to his Disciples, he said to them: I'm not a divider, am I?

Luke 12:13 Someone in the crowd said to him, Teacher, tell my brother to divide the family inheritance with me. 14 But he said to him, Friend, who set me to be a judge or arbitrator over you? 15 And he said to them, Take care! Be on your guard against all kinds of greed; for one's life does not consist in the abundance of possessions.

73. Jesus said: The harvest is indeed plentiful, but the workers are few. Ask the Lord to send workers for the harvest.

Matthew 9:37 Then he said to his disciples, The harvest is plentiful, but the laborers are few; 38 therefore ask the Lord of the harvest to send out laborers into his harvest.

74. He said: Lord, there are many around the well, yet there is nothing in the well. How is it that many are around the well and no one goes into it?

75. Jesus said: There are many standing at the door, but only those who are alone are the ones who will enter into the Bridal Chamber.

Matthew 22:14 For many are called, but few are chosen.

76. Jesus said: The Kingdom of the Father is like a rich merchant who found a pearl. The merchant was prudent. He sold his fortune and bought the one pearl for himself. You also, seek for his treasure which does not fail, which endures where no moth can come near to eat it nor worm to devour it.

Matthew 13:45 Again, the kingdom of heaven is like a merchant in search of fine pearls; 46 on finding one pearl of great value, he went and sold all that he had and bought it.

Matthew 6:19 Do not store up for yourselves treasures on earth, where moth and rust consume and where thieves break in and steal; 20 but store up for yourselves treasures in heaven, where neither moth nor rust consumes and where thieves do not break in and steal.

77. Jesus said: "I-Am" the Light who is over all things, "I-Am" the All. From me all came forth and to me all return (The All came from me and the All has come to me). Split wood, there am I. Lift up the stone and there you will find me.

John 8:12 Again Jesus spoke to them, saying, I am the light of the world. Whoever follows me will never walk in darkness but will have the light of life.

John 1:3 All things came into being through him, and without him not one thing came into being.

78. Jesus said: Why did you come out to the wilderness; to see a reed shaken by the wind? And to see a person dressed in fine (soft – plush) garments like your rulers and your dignitaries? They are clothed in plush garments, and they are not able to recognize (understand) the truth.

Matthew 11:7 As they went away, Jesus began to speak to the crowds about John: What did you go out into the wilderness to look at? A reed shaken by the wind? 8 What then did you go out to see? Someone dressed in soft robes? Look, those who wear soft robes are in royal palaces. 9 What then did you go out to see? A prophet? Yes, I tell you, and more than a prophet.

79. A woman from the multitude said to him: Blessed is the womb which bore you, and the breasts which nursed you! He said to her: Blessed are those who have heard the word (meaning) of the Father and have truly kept it. For there will be days when you will say: Blessed be the womb which has not conceived and the breasts which have not nursed.

Luke 11:27 While he was saying this, a woman in the crowd raised her voice and said to him, Blessed is the womb that bore you and the breasts that nursed you! 28 But he said, Blessed rather are those who hear the word of God and obey it!

Luke 23:29 For the days are surely coming when they will say, Blessed are the barren, and the wombs that never bore, and the breasts that never nursed.

80. Jesus said: Whoever has come to understand (recognize) the world (world system) has found a corpse, and whoever has found the corpse, of him the world (world system) is not worthy.

81. Jesus said: Whoever has become rich should reign, and let whoever has power renounce it.

82. Jesus said: Whoever is close to me is close to the fire, and whoever is far from me is far from the Kingdom.

83. Jesus said: Images are visible to man but the light which is within them is hidden. The light of the father will be revealed, but he (his image) is hidden in the light.

84. Jesus said: When you see your reflection, you rejoice. Yet when you perceive your images which have come into being before you, which neither die nor can be seen, how much will you have to bear?

85. Jesus said: Adam came into existence from a great power and a great wealth, and yet he was not worthy of you. For if he had been worthy, he would not have tasted death.

86. Jesus said: The foxes have their dens and the birds have their nests, yet the Son of Man has no place to lay his head for rest.

Matthew 8:20 And Jesus said to him, Foxes have holes, and birds of the air have nests; but the Son of Man has nowhere to lay his head.

87. Jesus said: Wretched is the body which depends upon another body, and wretched is the soul which depends on these two (upon their being together).

88. Jesus said: The angels and the prophets will come to you, and what they will give you belongs to you. And you will give them what you have, and said among yourselves: When will they come to take (receive) what belongs to them?

89. Jesus said: Why do you wash the outside of your cup? Do you not understand (mind) that He who creates the inside is also He who creates the outside?

Luke 11:39 Then the Lord said to him, Now you Pharisees clean the outside of the cup and of the dish, but inside you are full of greed and wickedness. 40 You fools! Did not the one who made the outside make the inside also?

90. Jesus said: Come unto me, for my yoke is comfortable (natural) and my lordship is gentle— and you will find rest for yourselves.

Matthew 11:28 Come to me, all you that are weary and are carrying heavy burdens, and I will give you rest. 29 Take my yoke upon you, and learn from me; for I am gentle and humble in heart, and you will find rest for your souls. 30 For my yoke is easy, and my burden is light.

91. They said to him: Tell us who you are, so that we may believe in you. He said to them: You examine the face of the sky and of the earth, yet you do not recognize Him who is here with you, and you do not know how to seek in (to inquire of Him at) this moment (you do not know how to take advantage of this opportunity).

John 9:36 He answered, And who is he, sir? Tell me, so that I may believe in him.

Luke 12:54 He also said to the crowds, When you see a cloud rising in the west, you immediately say, It is going to rain; and so it happens. 55 And when you see the south wind blowing, you say, There will be scorching heat; and it happens. 56 You hypocrites! You know how to interpret the appearance of earth and sky, but why do you not know how to interpret the present time?

92. Jesus said: Seek and you will find. But in the past I did not answer the questions you asked. Now I wish to tell them to you, but you do not ask about (no longer seek) them.

Matthew 7:7 Ask, and it will be given you; search, and you will find; knock, and the door will be opened for you.

93. Jesus said: Do not give what is sacred to the dogs, lest they throw it on the dung heap. Do not cast the pearls to the swine, lest they cause it to become dung (mud).

Matthew 7:6 Do not give what is holy to dogs; and do not throw your pearls before swine, or they will trample them under foot and turn and maul you.

94. Jesus said: Whoever seeks will find. And whoever knocks, it will be opened to him.

Matthew 7:8 For everyone who asks receives, and everyone who searches finds, and for everyone who knocks, the door will be opened.

95. Jesus said: If you have money, do not lend at interest, but rather give it to those from whom you will not be repaid.

Luke 6:34 If you lend to those from whom you hope to receive, what credit is that to you? Even sinners lend to sinners, to receive as much again. 35 But love your enemies, do good, and lend, expecting nothing in return. Your reward will be great, and you will be children of the Most High; for he is kind to the ungrateful and the wicked.

96. Jesus said: The Kingdom of the Father is like a woman who has taken a little yeast and hidden it in dough. She produced large loaves of it. Whoever has ears, let him hear!

Matthew 13:33 He told them another parable: The kingdom of heaven is like yeast that a woman took and mixed in with three measures of flour until all of it was leavened.

97. Jesus said: The Kingdom of the Father is like a woman who was carrying a jar full of grain. While she was walking on a road far from home, the handle of the jar broke and the grain poured out behind her onto the road. She did not know

it. She had noticed no problem. When she arrived in her house, she set the jar down and found it empty.

98. Jesus said: The Kingdom of the Father is like someone who wished to slay a prominent person. While still in his own house he drew his sword and thrust it into the wall in order to test whether his hand would be strong enough. Then he slew the prominent person.

99. His Disciples said to him: Your brethren and your mother are standing outside. He said to them: Those here who do my Father's desires are my Brethren and my Mother. It is they who will enter the Kingdom of my Father.

Matthew 12:46 While he was still speaking to the crowds, his mother and his brothers were standing outside, wanting to speak to him. 47 Someone told him, Look, your mother and your brothers are standing outside, wanting to speak to you. 48 But to the one who had told him this, Jesus replied, Who is my mother, and who are my brothers? 49 And pointing to his disciples, he said, Here are my mother and my brothers! 50 For whoever does the will of my Father in heaven is my brother and sister and mother.

100. They showed Jesus a gold coin, and said to him: The agents of Caesar extort taxes from us. He said to them: Give the things of Caesar to Caesar, give the things of God to God, and give to me what is mine.

Mark 12:14 Is it lawful to pay taxes to the emperor, or not? 15 Should we pay them, or should we not? But knowing their hypocrisy, he said to them, Why are you putting me to the test? Bring me a denarius and let me see it. 16 And they brought one. Then he said to them, Whose head is this, and whose title? They answered, The emperor's. 12:17 Jesus said to them, Give to the emperor the things that are the emperor's, and to God the things that are God's. And they were utterly amazed at him.

101. Jesus said: Whoever does not hate his father and his mother as I do, will not be able to become my Disciple. And whoever does not love his Father and his Mother as I do, will not be able to become my Disciple. For my mother bore me, yet my true Mother gave me the life.

Matthew 10:37 Whoever loves father or mother more than me is not worthy of me; and whoever loves son or daughter more than me is not worthy of me.

102. Jesus said: Damn these Pharisees. They are like a dog sleeping in the feed trough of oxen. For neither does he eat, nor does he allow the oxen to eat.

Matthew 2:.13 But woe unto you, scribes and Pharisees, hypocrites! because you shut the kingdom of heaven against men; for you neither enter yourselves, nor allow those who would enter to go in.

103. Jesus said: Blessed is the person who knows at what place of the house the bandits may break in, so that he can rise and collect his things and prepare himself before they enter.

Matthew 24:43 But understand this: if the owner of the house had known in what part of the night the thief was coming, he would have stayed awake and would not have let his house be broken into.

104. They said to him: Come, let us pray today and let us fast. Jesus said: What sin have I committed? How have I been overcome (undone)? When the Bridegroom comes forth from the Bridal Chamber, then let them fast and let them pray.

105. Jesus said: Whoever acknowledges (comes to know) father and mother, will be called the son of a whore.

106. Jesus said: When you make the two one, you will become Sons of Man (children of Adam), and when you say to the mountain: Move! It will move.

Mark 11:23 Truly I tell you, if you say to this mountain, Be taken up and thrown into the sea, and if you do not doubt in your heart, but believe that what you say will come to pass, it will be done for you.

107. Jesus said: The Kingdom is like a shepherd who has a hundred sheep. The largest one of them went astray. He left the ninety-nine and sought for the one until he found it. Having searched until he was weary, he said to that sheep: I desire you more than the ninety-nine.

Matthew 18:12 What do you think? If a shepherd has a hundred sheep, and one of them has gone astray, does he not leave the ninety-nine on the mountains and go in search of the one that went astray? 13 And if he finds it, truly I tell you, he rejoices over it more than over the ninety-nine that never went astray.

108. Jesus said: Whoever drinks from my mouth will become like me. I will become him, and the secrets will be revealed to him.

109. Jesus said: The Kingdom is like a person who had a treasure hidden in his field and knew nothing of it. After he died, he bequeathed it to his son. The son accepted the field knowing nothing of the treasure. He sold it. Then the person who bought it came and plowed it. He found the treasure. He began to lend money at interest to whomever he wished.

Matthew 13:44 The kingdom of heaven is like treasure hidden in a field, which someone found and hid; then in his joy he goes and sells all that he has and buys that field.

110. Jesus said: Whoever has found the world (system) and becomes wealthy (enriched by it), let him renounce the world (system).

Mark 10:21 Then Jesus beholding him loved him, and said unto him, One thing thou lackest: go thy way, sell whatsoever thou hast, and give to the poor, and thou shalt have treasure in heaven: and come, take up the cross, and follow me. 22 And he was sad at that saying, and went away grieved: for he had great possessions. 23 And Jesus looked round about, and saith unto his disciples, How hardly shall they that have riches enter into the kingdom of God!

111. Jesus said: Heaven and earth will roll up before you, but he who lives within the Living-One will neither see nor fear death. For, Jesus said: Whoever finds himself, of him the world is not worthy.

112. Jesus said: Damned is the flesh which depends upon the soul. Damned is the soul which depends upon the flesh.

113. His Disciples said to him: When will the Kingdom come? Jesus said: It will not come by expectation (because you watch or wait for it). They will not say: Look here! or:

Look there! But the Kingdom of the Father is spread upon the earth, and people do not realize it.

Luke 17:20 And when he was demanded of by the Pharisees, when the kingdom of God should come, he answered them and said, The kingdom of God cometh not with observation: Neither shall they say, Lo-Here! Lo-There! For, behold, the kingdom of God is within you.

(Saying 114 was written later and was added to the original text.)

114. Simon Peter said to them: Send Mary away from us, for women are not worthy of this life. Jesus said: Behold, I will draw her into me so that I make her male, in order that she herself will become a living spirit like you males. For every female who becomes male will enter the Kingdom of the Heavens.

Tao Te Ching

1

The Tao that can be explained is not the eternal Tao
The name that can be spoken is not the eternal Name.

The unspeakable is the beginning of everything.
Naming is the origin of every separate thing.

Free from desire, you realize the mystery.
Trapped in desire, you only see the manifestations.

Mystery and manifestations
Arise from the same source.

It is experienced as darkness.
Darkness within darkness.
The gateway to all understanding.

2

When beautiful things appear as beautiful,
It is because other things are called ugly.

We can only know Good because there is Evil.

Having and not having are born together
Being and not being arise from each other.
Difficult and easy support each other.
Long and short define each other.

High and low depend on each other.
Sound and silence harmonize each other.
Before and after follow each other.

Therefore the Master acts without doing anything
And teaches without talking.

He allows things to come and go naturally.
He does not hold on.
He has but doesn't possess, works but takes no credit,
He has no expectations.

It is done and then forgotten, therefore, it lasts forever.

3

If you give some men power, others become powerless.
If you assign value, people begin to steal.
Desire begets confusion of the heart.

The Master leads by emptying people's minds
And filling their hearts,
By weakening their ambition
And toughening their resolve.
He helps people lose everything they know and desire.

Craftiness, ambition, and expectations
Cause things to go badly.
Practice not-doing, and everything will be well.

4

The Tao is like an empty well; used but never emptied.
It is the eternal void and source of all possibilities.

It blunts the sharpness, untangles the knot;
Softens the glare, unifies the dust.

It is hidden deeply but is ever-present.
I don't know from where it came.
It is older than God.

5

The Tao is impartial;
It gives birth to both good and evil.
The Master is impartial
He sees people as both good and evil.

The Tao is like a bellows:
It is empty, changeable, potential in form.
The more it is moved, the more it yields.
The more you talk of it, the less your words count.

Hold on to the stillness of the center.

6

The Tao is called the Great Mother:
Empty yet inexhaustible,
It gives birth to all things.
It is always present within you.
If you use it; it will never fail.

7

Tao is eternal.
Why is it eternal?
It was never born;
Thus, it can never die.

The Master stays behind;
That is why he is ahead.
He is detached from all things;
That is why he is one with all things.

Because he has let go of himself,
He attains fulfillment.

8

The highest good is like water,
Which nourishes all things without trying.
It is content with the low places that people disdain.
Water, goodness and the Tao flow in the same way.

In dwelling, be close to the land.
In thinking, go deep within the heart.
In conflict, be fair and generous.
When speaking, be true.

When ruling, be fair
In work, be competent.
In life, be completely present in each moment.

If there is no fight, there will be no blame.

9

Better to stop short than to fill your bowl to overflowing.
The sharpened knife dulls easily.
Collect money, jewels, and possessions
And you cannot protect them.
Gather wealth and position
And your heart will be their captive.

Do your work, then let it go.
This is the only path to inner peace.

10

Can you control your mind and
Keep it from wandering?
Can you keep your oneness and focus?
Can you let your body become
Supple as a newborn child's?

Can you cleanse your inner vision?
Can you love people and lead them
Without guile or will?
Can you deal with the most vital matters
By letting events take their course?

Can you be lead by Tao,
Keeping an empty mind
And thus being open to all things?

Are you able to be still,
Give birth and nourish,
Create and bear without possessing,
Act without expectations,
Lead without controlling?

This is the highest virtue.

11

Thirty spokes join at the hub of a wheel.
It is the center hole that has use.

We shape clay into a pot.
It is the emptiness inside

That makes it useful.

Shape doors and windows for a house.
It is the space that makes it useful.

We derive benefit from things that are there
And usefulness from what is not there.

12

Five colors blind the eye.
Five sounds deafen the ear.
Five flavors dull the taste.
Racing thoughts confuse the mind.
Desires lead the heart astray.

The Master observes the world
But is guided by his intuition.
He allows things to come and go
As they will.

▓▓

13

Disgrace and success are the same.
Misfortune is a condition of life.

What does it mean to accept disgrace willingly?
Accept not being important.
Do not be concerned with loss or gain.

What does it mean to accept misfortune
As a condition of life?
Misfortune comes to all who are born.
If you had no body, what misery would you have?

Submit to the Tao and you will be trusted with everything.
Love the world as yourself and you can care for all beings.

14

Look for it, and it can't be seen.
Listen for it, and it can't be heard.
Grasp for it, and it can't be held.
These three are beyond understanding,
Thus they as joined as one.

Above, it isn't bright.
Below, it isn't dark.
It is an unbroken, unnamable thread
That returns to the nothingness.
The form is void.
Image without visage,
Beyond definition and imagination.

Examine it. You will see no beginning;
Follow it and there is no end.
With the ancient Tao you will be in the eternal present.
Knowing the beginning is the essence of wisdom.

15

The ancient Masters were profound and subtle.
The depth of their wisdom cannot be measured.
Because they cannot be recognized
We can only describe their appearance.

They were careful
As someone crossing an ice covered stream,
Alert like a warrior in hostile territory,
Courteous as a guest,
Yielding as melting ice,

Simple as a block of wood,
Receptive as a valley,
Clear as a pool of water.

Can you be still inside while the mud settles?
Can you wait quietly until the moment is right?

The Master doesn't seek fulfillment.
Without seeking and without expectations
He is not confused by desires.

16

Empty your mind of every thought.
Let your mind and heart still.
Watch things come and go without attachment.

Everything grows, matures,
And returns to the same source.
Returning to the source is stillness and peace.
This is the way of nature.
It is the way of Tao and it is unchanging.

Not knowing the consistency of Tao
Leads to confusion and disaster.
When you realize the common source

You become tolerant and charitable.
Giving to others, you will be as a king.
Being as a king, you will become divine.
Being divine, you will become one with the eternal Tao.

When death comes, you will be ready
For you will know that the Tao will never pass away.

17

When the Master governs,
The people are hardly aware that he exists.
An ineffective leader is known and loved.
A poor leader is feared.
The worst is one who is despised.

If you don't trust the people, you will not be trusted.
If you do not trust, you make others untrustworthy.

The Master says nothing.
When work is done
The people say, We did it all!

18

When the great Tao is forgotten,
Goodness and piety arise.

When the cleverness and knowledge begin
Falseness and pretension are born.

When there is no peace in the family,
Filial piety and devotion begin.
When the country falls into disarray,
Patriotism is born.

19

Give up trying to be holy or wise,
And people will be a hundred times happier.
Throw away ideas of kindness, morality, and justice,
And people will rediscover love and family.
Give up industriousness and profit,
And there won't be any robbers or thieves.
These three are outward forms and are useless.

Cultivate simplicity.
Realize your true nature.
Renounce selfishness.
Do not desire.

20

Stop thinking, and end your troubles.
What is the difference between yes and no?
What is the difference between success and failure?
Why must I fear what others fear? How ridiculous!

Other people are content with a feast or party
Others are content with a park in spring or a beautiful view.
I alone wonder, uncaring, expressionless as a newborn child.
I have no home.
Other people have what they need;

I alone have nothing.
Others are clear and witty.
I am nothing. My mind is empty.

Other people are bright;
I alone am dim.
Other people are clever;
I alone am dull.
Other people have a purpose;
I am aimless and depressed,
Drifting like a wave on the ocean,
Blown by the wind.

I am different from the others.
I am nourished from the Great Mother.

21

The Master keeps his own mind
And is alone, always at one with the Tao.

The Tao cannot be imagined, yet within is image.
It is elusive and formless, yet within is form.

The Tao is dark and void, yet within is radiance.
The essence is real, yet within is faith.

Since before time was and until now, the Tao is.
How do I know the way of creation is true?
Because of this; I look inside myself and it is there.

22

Yield and overcome;
Bend and be straight;
If you want to become full,
Let yourself be empty.
If you want to be reborn,

Let yourself die.
If you want to be fulfilled,
Give up everything.

Therefore, the Master, resides in the Tao,
And thus sets an example for all.
Because he doesn't put on a display,
People can see his true light.
Because he does not boast,
People can trust his words.
Because he doesn't know who he is,
People recognize themselves in him.
Not bragging or boasting,
There is no quarrel or dissention.

The ancient Masters said,
If you want to receive all,
Give up everything,
Be complete and all things will be yours.

23

To talk a little is natural.
High winds and heavy rains soon exhaust themselves.
If Heaven and Earth cannot sustain then how can man?

He who lives the Tao,
Is in unity with the Tao
He who lives virtuously experiences virtue.
If you lose the Way,
You are willingly lost.

Trust your natural responses;
And everything will be as it should.

24

He who stands on tiptoe is not steady.
He who strives cannot maintain the pace.
He who wishes to be known is not enlightened.
He who defines himself cannot know his true nature.
He who lords over others cannot empower himself.
He who brags will not be remembered.
According to followers of Tao,
These are extra food and unnecessary baggage.
They weigh you down, slow you down and impede your joy.
The followers of Tao reject them.

25

There was something formless and mysterious
Born before anything existed.
It is silent, peaceful, and empty.
Solitary. Unchanging.
Eternally present – peace within motion.
It is the mother of the all things.
It is unnamable.
I call it the Tao.

It flows through all things,
And then returns.

The Tao is great.
The sky is great.
Earth is great.
Man is great.
These are the four great powers.

Man follows the Earth.
Earth follows the sky.
The sky follows the Tao.
The Tao follows only its own natural way.

26

The heavy is the root of the light.
The still is the master of all that moves.

Thus the Master travels all day
Without leaving "home."
However splendid the views,
He stays unattached and calm.

Why should the lord of a country
Flit about like a fool?
If you let yourself be quixotic,
You lose your root.
To be restless or anxious,
Is to lose control and move too soon.

27

A good traveler leaves no tracks.
A good speaker does not stutter.
A good mathematician needs no paper.
A good door needs no lock yet cannot be opened.
A good binding needs no knots yet cannot be untied.

Thus the Master cares for all people
And doesn't reject anyone.
He nurtures all and abandons nothing.
This is called embodying the light.

What is a good man but a bad man's teacher?
What is a bad man but a good man's responsibility?
The teacher is to be respected,
And the student is to be nurtured.
However intelligent you are, if you do not follow
This way there will be confusion.
This is the secret.

28

Know the strength of the masculine,
Yet keep the heart of the feminine:
Let all things flow through you,
Like a true and constant stream.
If you do this, the Tao will never forsake you
And you will be like a little child once more.

Know the white,
Yet keep the black:
Be an example for the world.
If you are an example for the world,

Like a true and constant stream.
You will return, flowing to the All.

Know honor,
Yet have no care for it:
Be the valley of the world.
Being the valley of the world,
All things will flow into you.

Return to the simple state of a block of wood.
Then you will be useful and full of potential.
When the Master uses the Tao he rises above the rest.
Thus a master tailor cuts little.

29

Do you want to improve the world?
I don't think it can be done.

The world is sacred.
It can't be improved.
If you tamper with it, you will ruin it.
If you treat it like a procession, you will lose it.
There are some that are ahead,
And some behind;
Some that are difficult;

And some that are easy;
Some that are weak,
And some that are strong;
Some that will endure,
And some that will be overthrown.

Seek the center path.
Avoid extremes and excess.
Seek balance.
The Master sees and accepts
Without trying to control.

30

If you counsel a warrior about the Tao
Tell him he should not use force.
For every force there is a reaction.
Briars grow where armies tread.
Famine follows in the wake of war.
Do only what needs to be done.
Never take advantage of power.

Achieve results but the results are not your own.
Do not let pride interfere.
Thus, there is nothing to brag about.

Nothing to be proud of.
Nothing to fight about.

Force is followed by weakness.
This is not the Way of the Tao.
Any other way will lead to premature destruction.

31

Weapons are the instruments of violence;
All decent men hate them.

Weapons are the instruments of fear;
A decent man will avoid them until there is no choice.
Peace and serenity are his highest desires.
Victory is no cause for celebration.
For, it you celebrate victory you celebrate death and defeat.
He cannot delight in the slaughter of men.

On happy occasions the underdog is celebrated.
On sad occasions people look to their leaders.
Generals stand to the left, kings and presidents to the right.
Therefore, war is conducted like a funeral
He enters a battle gravely, and has compassion for those killed,
As with a funeral.

32

The Tao cannot be defined.
It is smaller than anything formed,
And cannot be grasped.

If powerful men could use it all things would flow naturally.
Men would do as they should
And the rain would come in its season.

When the whole is divided, all parts must have a name.
Knowing when to stop you can avoid troubles.

All things end in the Tao
As rivers end at the sea.

33

Knowing others is intelligence;
Knowing yourself is wisdom.
Mastering others requires force;
Mastering yourself requires inner strength.

If you realize that you have enough,
You are truly rich.
Tenacity and a perfect finish require willpower.

He who stays centered will endure.
To live in the eternal present one will never die.

34

The great Tao flows everywhere.
All things are born from it and it holds nothing in reserve.
It creates naturally and is not possessive.
It pours itself into its work,
Yet it makes no claim.

It nourishes infinite worlds,
Yet it doesn't hold on to them.

Since it is merged with all things
And is hidden in their hearts,
It can be called humble.
Since all things vanish into it,
It alone endures.
It can be called great.
It isn't aware of its greatness;
Thus it is truly great.

35

All men seek he who is centered in the Tao.
There they find rest, joy, and peace of mind.

Music or the smell of good food
May entice people to stop and enjoy.
But conversations about Tao
Seem boring and bland.
When you look for it, it cannot be seen.
When you listen for it, it cannot be heard.
When you use it, it cannot be exhausted.

36

If you wish to diminish it, allow it to expand.
If you wish to end it, allow it to mature.
If you wish to bash it against the ground, first raise it up.
If you wish to take something, it must first be given.
This is called understanding the nature of things.

The soft overcomes hard.
Weak overcomes strong.
Stay in your element.
Hide your strength until it is needed.

37

The Tao does not strive, yet it leaves nothing undone.

If powerful men observe this Way
The whole world would be as it should be.
If they wanted to act, they would resume
Their simple, everyday lives,
In harmony and free of desire.
Then, there would be peace.

38

A good man does not try to be good. It comes from his heart.
A fool tries to be good but he it is not his natural way.
Therefore, a good man does not strive yet good comes from him.
A fool rushes about trying to act good but no good comes of it.

The kind man acts, kindness leaves nothing lacking.
When a just man acts,
There is judgment and things are left to do.
When the man of discipline follows, no one responds
Until he begins his enforcement.

When the Tao is lost, there is kindness.
When kindness is lost, there is justice.

When justice is lost, there is ritual.
Ritual is the corpse of true faith,
And the beginning of foolishness.

Therefore the Master looks deeply
And is not concerned with how things appear on the surface,

He examines the fruit and not the flower.
He dwells on what is real and not on appearances.

39

From Ancient times, all things arise from the One:
The sky is clear and complete.
The earth is solid and complete.
The spirit is strong and complete.
The valley is full and complete.
All things are alive, complete, and content.

When the Way is not followed,
The sky becomes tarnished,
The earth becomes wasteland,
The spirit is depleted,
Creatures become extinct.

The Master humbly follows the Way, yet seems noble.
He acts as a lowly servant and is thus raised in stature.
Rulers and men of authority feel orphaned, widowed, and alone.
This is humility.
Too much success draws attention like sounding chimes and
Rattling jade stones.

40

Returning is the movement of the Tao.
Yielding is the way of the Tao.

All things are born of that which is and was.
Being is born of nothingness.

41

When the seeker hears of the Tao,
He immediately begins to practice it.
When an average man hears of the Tao,
He thinks about it but does not practice it.
When a foolish man hears of the Tao, he laughs out loud.
If he didn't laugh, it wouldn't be the Tao.

Thus it is said:
The path into the light seems dark,
The path forward seems to go back,
The direct path seems prolonged,
The highest good seems empty.
Great purity seems sullied.
Depth of spirit seems inadequate.
True stability seems changeable,
Great talent matures in time.
The highest notes are beyond hearing.
The Tao is obscured and nameless.

It nourishes and completes all things.

42

The Tao created One.
One created Two.
Two created Three.
Three gives birth to all things.

All things carry the feminine
But demonstrate the masculine.
When masculine and feminine are balanced,
Harmony is achieved.

Ordinary men hate being deserted, abandoned, or alone.
But these are how the Master is described.
Embracing his solitude
He becomes aware that he is one with All.

43

The softest thing in the world overcomes the hardest thing.
That which has no substance enters where there is no space.
This shows the value of non-action.

Teaching without words, and acting without movement is the Master's way.

44

Fame or integrity: which is more important?
Integrity or wealth: which do you desire more?
Success or failure: which is more damaging?

If you are attached to processions you will suffer.
If you hoard you will lose.
Contentment assuages disappointment.
Know when to stop, avoid troubles, and remain forever satisfied.

45

Great accomplishments seem imperfect,
But, they continue to be useful.
True fullness seems lacking,
Yet, it is never emptied.

True straightness seems crooked.
True wisdom seems foolish.
True grace seems awkward.

If you are cold, move.
If you are warm, be still.
In stillness and peace, the order of the universe is established.

46

When Tao is present within a country,
Fine horses are free to fertilize the fields.
When Tao is missing in a country,
War horses are bred in the county side.

There is no greater fault than desire,
No worse goad than discontentment.
No greater shame than selfishness
He who realizes enough is enough will be fulfilled.

47

Without traveling you can know the world.
Without looking out of a window,
You can see the ways of the Tao.
The more you go outside yourself the less you understand.

The Master understands without traveling,
Sees the Way without looking,
Achieves without action.

48

In pursuit of knowledge, every day something is added.
In the pursuit of the Tao, every day something is dropped.
Less and less is needed until stillness is achieved.
When nothing is done, nothing is left undone.
If things are left alone they will take their own course.
If you interfere - chaos.

49

The Master has no mind of his own.
He serves the needs of others.

He is good to people who are good.
He is also good to people who are not good.
This is true goodness.

He has faith in people who are trustworthy.
He also has faith in people who are not trustworthy.
This is true trust.

The Master is quiet, timid and does not consider himself.
People do not understand him.
They look and listen even though
They think he behaves like a child

50

In the space of a lifetime,
One third follows the way of life,
One third follows the way of death
And one third follows nothing
And drift through life,
Having no purpose.

He who knows how to live in the Tao
Moves without fear or thought of his actions.
He will not be harmed because there is no place

For weapons or beasts to enter him.
If there is no fear of death,
The mind is clear and death has no place.

51

Everything in existence is an expression of the Tao.
The Tao nurtures them.
Unconsciously and spontaneously, they take on form.
They allow circumstances to shape them.
That is why everything honors the Tao.

The Tao gives birth to all things.
Its goodness nourishes them, protects them, and comforts them.
The Tao does not possess them.
The Tao does not boast of them.
The Tao has no expectations of them.
The Tao guides without interfering.
This is the highest good.

52

Tao is the mother and beginning of all things.
All things issue from it like children from their mother;
And all things return to it.

To know the maker is to know the creation.
Recognize the children and know the mother,
And free yourself from fear and sorrow.

Stay quiet, focus the mind and life will be peaceful.
Speak without thought, entertain desires,
Rush about and your heart will be troubled.

Seeing into darkness and detail is insight.
Yielding is strength.

Use your own light.
Inwardly lighting your own path is wisdom.
Consistence leads to perfection.

53

The center path is the main road.
If I have any sense I will walk the clear path.
But, people prefer the side roads,
Even though the main path is easiest.
Step left or right and things are out of balance.
Stay centered within the Tao.

When rulers demand too much
Common folks lose their land;

When rulers spend money, buy weapons, and distribute wealth
Some wear expensive clothing
Eat fine food, and have many possessions;
While others go hungry.
These rulers are robbers and thieves.
They do not follow the Tao.

54

Whoever is firmly planted in the Tao
Will not be uprooted.
Whoever embraces the Tao
Will not slip away.
His name will be honored
From generation to generation.

Cultivate goodness in your life
And you will become genuine.
Encourage goodness in your family
And your family will flourish.
Spread it throughout your country
And your country will be an example
To the rest of the world.

Let it be present in the universe
And it will be omnipresent.

First, there must be virtue in family, then village,
Then nation, then the world.

How do I know this is true?
By looking.

55

He who is in harmony with the Tao
Is like a newborn child.
Whose bones are soft, its muscles are weak,
Yet its grip is strong.
It doesn't know about sex
Yet its penis can stand erect.
It screams and cries all day long,
Yet never becomes hoarse.
It is in harmony with the Tao.

Harmony brings consistency.
Consistency brings enlightenment.

The Master's power is in his timing.
He lets all things happen without rush or desire;
So he does not exhaust his energies.
He never expects results;

So, he is never disappointed.
What does not follow the Tao will not endure.

56

Those who know don't speak of it.
Those who speak of it do not know it.

Close your mouth,
Guard your senses,
Blunt your sharpness,
Reduce complex problems to basic issues,
Soften your glare,
Let your dust settle.
This is the primal Oneness.

When there is oneness
We will not distinguish between friend or enemy,
Gain or harm, honor or failure.
We will give ourselves continually.

This is the highest state of being.

57

If you want to be a great leader,
You must learn to rule justly.
Do not try to control, allow plans to change on their own.
Rule without striving.

The more laws enacted,
The more cunning people will become.
The more violent the weapons,
The less secure people will be.
The more cunning the people are
The more difficult it is to solve the crimes.

Therefore the Master says:
I let go of the law and ritual,
And people become honest and peaceful.

I do not wage war, and people become prosperous,
I let go of all desire to be a ruler
And the people become good and peaceful.

58

If a country is governed with tolerance,
The people are down to earth and honest.

If people are repressed, they become cunning and crafty.
When happiness is contrived, it is meaningless
Try to make people happy,
And the result is misery.
Try to legislate morality,
And you sow immorality and vice.

Thus the Master is intelligent but not cunning,
To the point but not hurtful.
Straightforward, but not rude.
Radiant, but not blinding.

59

For governing a country and serving the common good,
There is nothing better than moderation.

The moderation comes from laying aside your own ideas.
It depends on wisdom gathered through maturity.
If wisdom is acquired, nothing is impossible.
When possibilities are seen as limitless,
Then, a man is equipped to rule.

Nothing is impossible for him.
Because he has become the mother of all people.
He has deep and solid roots into the Tao.

He will nourish others and have a long, happy life.
He will be able to see the outcome from the beginning.

60

Governing a large country
Is like frying a small fish.
It breaks apart if poked too much.
Too much disturbance leads to damage.

Let Tao be the center
And evil will have no power over you.
Evil exists but can be avoided and does not propagate.

The Master avoids evil.
And thus protects both himself and others.

61

When a country obtains great power,
It becomes like the sea:
All streams run downward into it.
The more powerful it grows,
The greater the need for humility.
Yielding to a smaller country,

The greater country will absorb it.
If the smaller country yields to the greater country
It remains whole and can conquer from within.
Humility means trusting the Tao,
Thus, never needing to be defensive.
It is natural for the lesser to serve and the greater to lead.
It is Virtue for the greater to yield.

62

The Tao is the source of all things.
It is the good man's treasure,
And the bad man's refuge.

Honors can be bought with flattering words,
Respect can be won with good deeds;
The Tao does not choose,
So, do not abandon the bad man.
One day he could be king.
On that day, do not send gifts,
But instead, offer the Tao.

Why did the ancient ones esteem the Tao?
Because, when you seek, you find;
And when you make a mistake, you are forgiven.

Therefore, it is the greatest gift of all.

63

Act without striving;
Work without effort.
See the small as large
And the few as many.
Confront the bitter.
Simplify the complicated.
Attend to details.
Achieve greatness by
Accomplishing small feats.

By doing these things
You will do great things as if they were easy.

Great acts are made of small deeds.
The Master never attempts greatness;
Thus, he achieves greatness.

When there is difficulty, he is not concerned.
He has no preconceived ideas of how things should be.

64

What is rooted is easy to nourish.
What is first beginning is easily stopped.

What is brittle is easy to break.
What is small is easy to scatter.

Prevent trouble before it arises.
Put things in order before there is confusion.

The giant tree the size of a man's arm span
Grows from a small seedling.
A skyscraper begins with a pile of dirt.
The journey of a thousand miles
Starts from beneath your feet.

Rushing into action, you are defeated from the start.
Trying to grasp things, they will slip through your fingers.

Therefore the Master takes no action.
Letting things unfold, he is not defeated.
He does not try to hold anything,
Thus by claiming nothing, he has nothing to lose.

People fail when nearing the end.
The finish should be as strong as the beginning.
Then there will be no failure.

What he desires is non-desire;
He owns nothing but collects nothing.
He has nothing but gives men All.

He helps others find their own nature.
He can care for all things by doing nothing but showing forth
the Tao.

65

The ancient Masters
Didn't try to educate the people.
They kept knowledge to themselves.

When people think they know the answers,
They are difficult to guide.
Rulers who use deceit cheat the country.
If you want to learn how to govern,
Avoid being clever or deceitful.
The simplest pattern is the clearest
And easiest to follow.

Cleverness or simplicity; these are the two options.
Understanding this leads to goodness.
The highest good leads all men back to Tao.

66

All streams flow to the sea.
Because it is lower
It receives and rules ten thousand streams.

If the Master would lead,
He must place himself humbly below them.
If you want to lead,
You must learn how to follow.

If a ruler serves the people
No one feels oppressed.
If he stands before the people to guide them,
No one feels manipulated.
The whole world is grateful to him and will not tire of him.
Because he does not compete
He meets with no resistance.

67

Some say that my teaching of the Tao cannot be understood.
Others call it lofty but impractical.
It is different and thus has endured.

I have only three treasures to teach;
Simplicity, patience, and compassion.

Being simple in actions and in thoughts,
You return to the source of being.

Being patient with all,
You are in harmony with the Tao
And care not whether you are ahead or behind others.
In compassion you reconcile all beings and are yourself,
Reconciled.

Lack of compassion is not bravery.
Lack of patience is not spontaneity.
Lack of simplicity is not cleverness
To lack any of these things is certain death.

Compassion brings victory in battle and a steadfast defense.
Heaven saves and guards its own when there is compassion.

68

The best soldier is controlled and thoughtful.
The best general patiently searches the mind of his enemy.
The best businessman serves the good of his clients.
The best victor is merciful.

These embody the virtue of not striving.
They have the gift of knowing others
And thus knowing themselves.
This is in harmony with the Tao.

69

The generals have a saying:
He who moves first loses.
It is better to wait and see.
Better to retreat an inch
Than to take a foot by force.
But, where the enemy leaves an inch, I fill the void.

This is called going forward without seeming to advance;
Attacking without using weapons.

There is no greater misfortune
Than underestimating your enemy.

Underestimating your enemy means vilifying
And lessening him in your mind.

Thus you destroy your three treasures
And become your own worst enemy.

When the battle is joined,
He who is patient and yields, wins.

70

My teachings are easy to understand
And easy to perform.
Yet if you try to practice them you will fail.
If you grasp them they will slip away from you.

My teachings are older than the world.
My actions are from self-knowledge.
Men cannot understand these things
Because they do not seek them within.
Thus, I am abused and they are honored.

The Master wears simple clothes
And holds the treasure within him.

71

Not-knowing is true knowledge.
Ignoring this is sickness.
If you realize that you are sick;

You can start to become healthy.

The Master is sick of being sick
Thus, he has become well.

72

When they lose their sense of awe and mystery,
People turn to religion and law.

When they no longer trust,
If you visit, they are suspicious.
If you offer them work,
They will be wary.
Self-confidence will fail,
And they will become dependant on authority.

Therefore the Master steps back,
So that people won't be confused.
He is not arrogant and does not need to rule.
He lets go and gets out of the way.

73

A brave and driven man will place life on the line.
A brave and patient man will value life.
Of these two, one is good and one is injurious.

Heaven favors certain attributes.
Even the Master does not know why.

The Tao does not try but it covers the whole world.
It asks no questions but is answered to by all.
It is not petitioned but supplies every need.
It has no observable goal but fulfills all that is required.

The Tao casts its net wider than the world.
Though the mesh is large, it holds and keeps all things.

74

If men are not afraid to die,
There is nothing that can stop them.

Law is upheld by fear of punishment.
But who wants to be the executioner?
If you take his place you will harm yourself.

It is like trying to take the place of a master carpenter.

If you use his tools,
You may cut your hand.

75

When taxes are too high, people go hungry.
When the government is too restrictive, people soon rebel.

When the price of life becomes too high,
People think of death more often.

Having little to live on, or few things to live for,

The value of life falls.

76

Men are born soft and supple;
Dead, they are stiff and hard.
Green plants are tender and pliant;
When they die they become brittle, brown, and dry.

Thus whoever is stiff and inflexible

Is a disciple of death.
Whoever is soft and yielding
Is a disciple of life.

A tree that will not bend will be broken.
Tactics of life should be fluid to meet changing circumstance.
Flow with change or meet defeat.
For the hard and unyielding will be broken.
The soft and yielding will prevail.

77

As the Tao acts, it is like the bending of a bow.
The high is bent downward;
The low is raised up.
It adjusts excess and deficiency of strength,
Measure, and status
And blends all into harmony and balance.

The Tao takes from those with more and gives
To those with less.
Man's ways are the opposite.
Man esteems those who are wealthy and shuns
Those with little.

Only the Tao gives what it has.

The Master produces without owning,
Works without credit, succeeds without plaudits.
He is not proud or arrogant.

78

Nothing in the world is as soft and yielding as water.
Yet it wears down the hard and inflexible.
Nothing can withstand it.

The weak overcomes strong;
Gentle overcomes the rigid.
Everyone knows this but few practice it.

Therefore the Master knows
That only he who takes on the hardship of the people
Is fit to rule them.

And he who does not shield himself from common disaster
Is fit to rule a country.

True words seem paradoxical.

79

After a fight, resentment remains.
It cannot be helped.

Therefore, the Master fulfills his promises,
Corrects his own mistakes,
And has no expectations of others.

When there is honor, one does his part.
When there is no honor, one makes demands.
The Tao is everywhere,
But it rests on the good man.

80

If a country has few inhabitants,
They enjoy their work,
They don't need complicated machinery,
They love their homes,
They aren't interested in travel.

There are wagons and boats left unused,
Armor that is never worn.
People enjoy their simple ways, food, and clothes.

They live in peace with their neighbor.
Dogs bark and roosters crow and all is heard for miles away.

They are content to grow old and die without
Straying from their ways.

81

True words are not pleasing;
Pleasing words are not true.
Wise men don't need to prove their point;
Men who push their point are fools.
Those who know they could be wrong are learned.
Those who are certain they know are ignorant.

The Master has no possessions.
He hoards nothing.
The more he gives, the more he has.
The more he serves, the happier he is.

The Tao pierces the heart but does not harm.
The Tao nourishes by letting go.

By not dominating, the Master's obligation is done.

BIBLIOGRAPHY

The Gospels and The Synoptic Problem; The Literary Relationship of Matthew, Mark, and Luke. By Dennis Bratcher

Gospel of Thomas, The Brill translation. By Guillamont, Puech, Quispel, Till and Al Masih.

Gospel of Thomas. Translations by Thomas O. Lambdin (Coptic version); B.P Grenfell & A.S. Hunt (Greek Fragments); Bentley Layton (Greek Fragments); Commentary by: Craig Schenk

The Gospel of Thomas. By Thomas O. Lambdin

Gospel of Thomas. By Elaine Pagels in The Gnostic Gospels (New York: Random House, 1979)

An Introduction to Gnosticism . The Gnostic Society Library and the Nag Hammadi Library; An Explanatory Translation by Stan Rosenthal

The Gnostic Gospels. By Elaine Pagels. Published by Random House

Lost Scriptures. By Bart D. Ehrman. Published by Oxford University Press, 2003

Tao Te Ching, An Interpolation. By Peter A. Merel

Tao Te Ching, The Raymond Blakney translation from Mountain Man Graphics.

Tao Te Ching; A Recent Translation. By Charles Muller

Tao Te Ching: A Translation in Progress. By Chad Hansen

Tao Te Ching: An Etymological Resource. By Rick Harbaugh

Tao Te Ching. By Lao Tzu, Translation by Gia-Fu Feng, Jane English

Tao Te Ching. Written by Lao-Tzu. From a translation by S. Mitchell. July 1995

The Tao-te Ching. By Lao-Tzu. Translated by James Legge

The Holy Bible. Revised Standard Version. Copyright 1946, 1952, 1973 by the National Council of Churches of Christ.

Holy Bible, King James Version. Zandervan Press

ABOUT THE AUTHOR

Joseph Lumpkin is the author of the books *Encounter the Warrior's Heart; The Warrior's Heart Revealed; Twelve Tribes of Mankind; Dark Night of the Soul – A Journey to the Heart of God;* and *The Lost Book of Enoch.* Joseph earned his Doctorate of Ministry from Battlefield Baptist Institute.

Further, Mr. Lumpkin is a distinguished martial artist and instructor. He is the founder of Shinsei Hapkido, a recognized Christian martial arts system. Joseph Lumpkin holds a 6th degree Black Belt in Hapkido; a 3rd degree Black Belt in Akayama Ryu JuJitsu, and 2nd degree Black Belts in Shotokan Karate and Kodokan Judo.

CPSIA information can be obtained
at www.ICGtesting.com
Printed in the USA
BVHW030831201019
561563BV00001B/96/P

9 780976 099260